MATERIAL WORLD

MATERIALS

at the
SHOPS

By

William Anthony

BookLife
PUBLISHING

©2019
BookLife Publishing
King's Lynn
Norfolk PE30 4LS
All rights reserved.
Printed in Malaysia.

A catalogue record for this book
is available from the British Library.

ISBN: 978-1-78637-448-6

Written by:
William Anthony

Edited by:
John Wood

Designed by:
Danielle Jones

CONTENTS

Words that look like this can be found in the glossary on page 24.

WE'RE LIVING
IN A MATERIAL WORLD

Have you ever thought about what things are made of? Everything at the shops is made of something: wood, paper, plastic, glass... These things are called materials.

Shops, and everything in them, are made using materials.

All materials have <u>properties</u>. We can describe a material using its properties, such as how hard or soft it is. Let's have a look at the materials in shops.

Hard

Strong

A MATERIAL SHOP

Think about being at the shops. Before you go in, you can see what's inside through the window. What material do you think the window is made of?

See-through

The window is made of glass. Glass is the perfect material for a shop window because it is transparent, or see-through, which means you can see everything inside the shop!

FACT FILE: GLASS

Transparent

Hard

Flat

Smooth

SHELVES

When you go into a shop, some things are stacked on shelves. What do you think shelves are made from?

Strong

Hard

Most shelves are made from steel, which is one of the strongest types of metal. Shelves are made from a strong material like steel so they can <u>support</u> lots of objects!

FACT FILE: STEEL

- Strong
- Smooth
- Hard
- Flat
- Heavy

TINS

Lots of food at the shops comes in tins. A long time ago, tins used to be made of... tin! Now they are made of aluminium (say: a-luh-min-ee-um) or steel, because it is cheaper.

Can you think of a type of food that comes in a tin?

Aluminium is a type of metal that is light and can be made very thin. It is easy to shape too, which makes it a good material for making tin cans.

FACT FILE:
ALUMINIUM

Light

Thin

Waterproof

CARTONS

Do you drink juice or milk from a carton? Did you know that cartons are made from two different materials?

Light

Waterproof

One material is cardboard, which is used because it is light and easy to shape. The cardboard is coated in a different material – either plastic or wax – to make it waterproof.

FACT FILE:
CARDBOARD

- Thin
- Light
- Flexible
- Smooth or Textured

NEWSPAPERS

Newspapers tell us what is happening all over the world. But did you know that they are made in an amazing way?

The writing is made from ink, which starts wet and then dries.

Newspapers are made of paper, which comes from trees. The trees are turned into a soupy <u>pulp</u>. The pulp is then squeezed into thin sheets to make paper.

FACT FILE: PAPER

- Thin
- Smooth
- Can Be Torn
- <u>Natural</u>

CLOTHES

Some shops sell clothes, such as t-shirts and jumpers. Clothes can be made from different materials. Some materials can keep you warm and others can keep you cool.

Jumpers are made from a thick material, which keeps you warm.

Two <u>common</u> materials for clothes are cotton and wool. Cotton grows on cotton plants. Natural wool is made from a sheep's <u>fleece</u>.

FACT FILE: COTTON

- Thin
- Soft
- Natural

FACT FILE: WOOL

- Springy
- Soft
- Natural

BASKETS

When you're walking around the shop, you can use a basket to make it easier to carry lots of things. What properties do you think a basket needs to have?

Strong

Hard

Your basket needs to be light enough to carry, but strong and hard enough to put lots of things in. Plastic has all of these properties, so that's why it is normally used to make baskets.

FACT FILE:
PLASTIC

Hard

Strong

Light

19

MONEY

We can pay for shopping with coins, notes or a card. Coins are made of metal. Notes are made of paper or plastic. Cards are made of plastic and metal.

Some countries, like the UK, use plastic notes because you can't tear them.

We keep money in wallets and purses, which are often made of leather. Leather is made from animal skin.

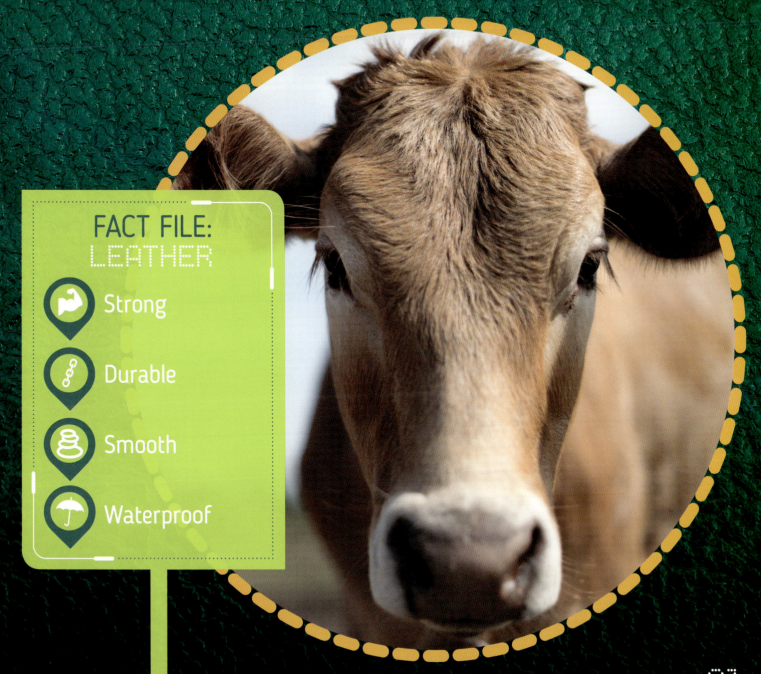

FACT FILE:
LEATHER

Strong

Durable

Smooth

Waterproof

MATERIAL MAGIC

Did you know that lots of the things you buy at the shops can be used again? Objects like old clothes, paper, cardboard and metal can be made into new materials. This is called recycling.

Recycling is good for our planet!

AT THE SHOPS

When you next go to the shops, see if you can find any materials that have some of the following properties...

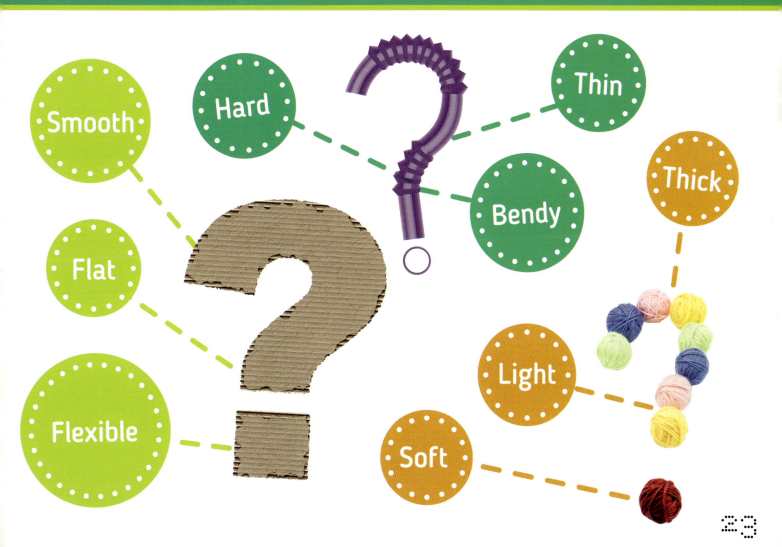

Smooth

Hard

Thin

Flat

Bendy

Thick

Flexible

Light

Soft

GLOSSARY

common	can be seen or found a lot
durable	not easily broken or worn out
fleece	the woolly, fluffy coat of a sheep
flexible	easily bends
natural	found in nature, not man-made
properties	ways of describing a material
pulp	a soft, wet, runny mixture
support	to hold up, assist or bear weight
waterproof	stops water or other liquids getting through

INDEX